MARRIED TO THE
MUSE

POEMS

Enjoy!
Jill Kelly

ALSO BY JILL KELLY

Poetry

So Much Is Beautiful, So Much Is Broken:
Poems from the Pandemic

Fiction

The Color of Longing

When Your Mother Doesn't

Fog of Dead Souls

Broken Boys

Ben Three Years Later

When the Past Comes Calling: Six Guys, One Girl, One Night

The House of Expectations

Nonfiction

Sober Truths: The Making of an Honest Woman

Sober Play: Using Creativity for a More Joyful Recovery

Candy Girl: How I Gave Up Sugar
and Created a Sweeter Life Between Meals

MARRIED TO THE
MUSE

POEMS

JILL KELLY

Flower vector art: Shutterstock/Ulyana Mo

Cover and book design by
Amy Livingstone, Sacred Art Studio
sacredartstudio.net

Cover photo and interior photos by the author.
jillkellycreative.com

ISBN: 9798386504526

DEDICATION

To all the women who marry the muse.

SOME WAYS I GOT HERE

FIRST BITE OF THE APPLE

My Indian princess is 7 like me.
Long red curls. Giggles when I
pin her to the bed. Me the bold
cavalry captain. She giggles more
when I kiss her.

The lamplight falls over us, halo of
blessing on a rainy winter afternoon
in the narrow attic.

What are you doing?

My Methodist mother stands huge
in the doorway, the bright overhead
bulb her sidekick of shame.

The buffalo no longer thunders
past the thin walls of the teepee.
My tongue forks for the first time.

Nothing.

Alison gets her coat, goes home. I wait
in the halo of the lamp for my father
and the hairbrush.

BRUISING TO BE FREE

The Pony Man came around one spring
with his camera and a western outfit.
No ride down the block. Just a sit and a pose.
The vest over my dress, the hat on my Dutch girl hair.

I never wanted to be a cowgirl.
I was always the wild horse
galloping across the unmown grass
when we were let loose for recess.

When I was caught and ridden
under the milk-white winter sky
by Kathy or Buster, the jump rope
left bruises on my waist from
straining to be free.

The Pony Man came back the next
week with the photo. $1. I still have it.

BLESSING OF THE BOOKMOBILE

I sit on the second step of the wide white
porch of the Skamania General Store. Three
cars in the gravel lot, motors running. I've been
waiting since Wednesday, my weekly supply
used up. I always come early. I need an injection
of the unknown, some other place to be.

Since I turned eight, I can come alone
down the steep drive to the highway, left
on the shoulder, nothing between our road
and the store but a hillside of weeds and a ditch
that runs wild with rain. This morning the log trucks
don't rumble by, and the sawmill is quiet.

I walk out to the highway but the road west is still
empty. I stand there, waiting for three toots of the horn,
the station wagon pulling its Airstream of salvation.

FOR MY SISTER, WHO REMEMBERS NOTHING

That shrouded summer house comes in my dreams,
dragging with it the treacherous winter when we inched
across the planks of the veranda slick with ice, our little
boots echoing, our mittened hands held tight.

In the dreams, I lie awake across the room from you, cold
beds piled with musty quilts, bare windows rimed with frost.
The fear shivers me, shocks me as it did when I was nine
and you were six.

It wasn't meant to be a prison nor Mom the jailer. But
she vanished each night with the oil lamp, locked us in
against a rumored stranger off the highway. No room for us
in the in-laws' tiny flat where she slept with the baby.

I didn't have the courage to hold you close in those endless
nights. In the dreams, I can't hold myself close either. I can
only lie frozen. Watch for that stranger. Pretend we aren't
there alone. Ache for the lamp to come back.

I'D LOST TRUST SO LONG BEFORE

Squinting in the spring sun despite
the wide-brimmed woman's hat,
my child self stands on the porch on 30th Street.
Around my shoulders a fox stole, its teeth
snapped shut on its tail for eternity.
My mother's handbag, black patent,
dwarfs my arm, its clasp as big as my hand.
Perfume wafts off the photograph: *Je reviens*
on a white hanky with yellow tatting.
The hat, the purse from the big box
of dress-up clothes, so big we could
fall into it.

The face in the photo smiles, a little shy,
the animal eyes wary.

WHAT PRICE BEAUTY

The torture was systematic.

Forced into a wooden chair
under the harsh overhead,
held down by maternal decree.
The pink and white chicken bones,
tissue-wrapped, soaked in tear gas.
My nose ran, my eyes too.
My neck ached.

The first time I was fooled,
thought it would make me cute,
make me somebody.
All it did was make me stink.

If I'd known the word,
I've had said *Fuck this*
even if it had meant
no TV for a month.

THE DAY OF MY BROTHER'S WEDDING

Stiff turquoise satin, tight skirt,
    French twist sprayed stiffer than the dyed-to-match shoes.
      Hippie self erased.

Hours earlier. Gin and tonic in hand
    my mother lies in the hotel tub.
      Fix me another, will you, honey?

She hands me the glass, cubes clinking.
    Drink delivered, I hesitate on the edge of the tub. Then:
      I've fallen in love. We want to move to Europe.

She gives me that look. Ice Queen. Medusa.
    Spits out disbelief, disdain.
      Don't be silly. Who is this guy? You're not having sex, are you.

I've no time for this.
    She downs the drink.
      Holds out the glass.

WHAT IS THERE TO SAY

She secrets me into the kitchen.
Pulls out three tiny steno pads,
ones that fit in a palm, a pocket, a purse.
Each cover numbered: 1946, 47, 48.

I read fast, fascinated. Halfway through
the first, she clutches my arm, gin whispers:
See how difficult my life was?

She picks up another, reads from it:
Is John with F? He came in late,
smelling of whiskey and perfume.

I knew of my father's affairs.
Knew she couldn't confront him.
Knew I couldn't either.
My own sex life was casual.
It was the 70s.

We hear the recliner creak, TV go mute.
My mother slides them between cookbooks.
Gets out the ice and the gin.

OH, THE SEPTEMBER LIGHT

Its honey pours over the porch, sweetens
my tea, lights up the lines in my hands
that are now my mother's.

Dead twenty-five years. I can move
closer to her now than when we could have
touched, our spirits less mired in habit.

Maybe our souls really are light. If so,
I want mine, I want hers to be this September
light, the honey a healing between us.

THE WEIGHT OF OLD LOVERS

Just over the Line in Oakland

How It Goes When It's Over

The Summer I Was Thirty

Addressing the Relationship

What I Didn't Know Yet

Bachianas Brasileiras 5

The Last Day of My Old Life

Janis Ian Was Right

JUST OVER THE LINE IN OAKLAND

July 1969. *Astral Weeks* comes on. I'm lying
with my lover in his room on Shattuck Avenue.

We're just over the line, Berkeley to Oakland,
and over a murmur of voices.

The Black Panthers and their headquarters.
We pass them in the parking lot, faces

not yet famous: Cleaver, Newton, Davis.
None of us sees the future.

Not man walking on the moon. Watergate.
Roe v. Wade. Not the violent endings. Theirs. Ours.

Right now it's just the violins and Van's voice.
His curious poetics and our bodies slick with sweat.

The murmur of voices below us,
voices we can't quite hear.

HOW IT GOES WHEN IT'S OVER

She stops at the cash register,
hoping he's there in a booth,
hoping he stands up to hold her.

He stops at the cash register,
late on purpose,
hoping she doesn't come.

She orders tea that goes untouched.
He orders pie and wolfs it down.

She's still hopeful,
repeats *I don't understand,*
repeats *I love you,*
repeats *We're so good together.*

He doesn't want any of this,
repeats *It's just not working,*
repeats *There's no one else,*
repeats *This isn't useful.*

She goes to the ladies' room,
fixes her sad face,
washes her swollen eyes,
cradles her torn heart.

He asks for the bill,
leaves cash,
a big tip.

THE SUMMER I WAS THIRTY

I rode my bike to work
in the cool Eugene mornings,
my lover still abed
in the big house on Fairmount.

A tedious day ahead. Clerical
work. Summer job between
terms. I didn't care. I lived
for the nights.

ADDRESSING THE RELATIONSHIP

212 Stratford, Houston
    Old grime so thick
    we painted right over it.
    I took to driving the freeway
    to escape his cold fury.

213 Stratford, Houston
    Office in the back,
    Tapestry on the speakers.
    He made the money;
    I kept house.

219 Stratford, Houston
    I dropped a carton of eggs
    in the shag-carpeted kitchen.
    He didn't find it funny. I did.
    Long silences.

107 Sul Ross, Houston
    A nice house, a nice yard.
    Grown-up living, grown-up drinking.
    He confessed his first adultery.
    I pretended it didn't hurt.

PO Box 612, North Umpqua Hwy, Oregon
    A year in the woods on unemployment.
    Too much bourbon, too much sleep.
    We talked of marriage,
    let the conversation drop.

3415 Bertlesen, Eugene
    One last try.
    Grad school, real estate.
    My turn to cheat.
    He kept the dogs, I took the cats.

WHAT I DIDN'T KNOW YET

The first of those ten summers together
I was happy. New love brought me into
my body. I showed it off in soft dresses:
red, teal blue.

Lazy nights, languorous mornings.
I had work, classes, but thought
only of him. His touch. His bed.
The long sunny days hid the shadows.

He grew flowers, brought me
dinner plate dahlias. Wrote
me love notes that I hung on to
for decades. Can you blame me?

We made love in his garden, his office,
on the beach, in the woods. We made
promises that meant the world to me
and little to him.

BACHIANAS BRASILEIRAS 5

You're on the redeye from Portland. You've had all the bourbon the attendant will sell you. You stuff your jealousy into the seat pocket and lean back. Your partner is meeting you, eager to show off his red Alfa, a midlife gift from a new lover.

Oblivion doesn't come, hard as you try.

You put on the free headphones, plug into piped-in choices. The third song, Villa-Lobos, undoes you, slowly unraveling what's sore and sorry. The cellos, the wordless soprano wrap you in tender chords.

From far off, your tormented heart hears a door opening.

THE LAST DAY OF MY OLD LIFE

I wake at 4:14. My body in need
yet my mind is clear. An unexpected
gift, for I am terrified, no bigger
change imaginable.

I'm up a while. The cats to feed.
Me too, a little something. I lay me
back down. Cheap chilled chablis
my companion. My refuge.

Mid-afternoon I rise, thinking of his last
words. *I can't drive you. I won't. I have
other plans.* No surprise there. None
of those left between us.

I shower. Pack. Tidy up. Even in those
last scary moments, *neat* still my mantra.
In the back of the fridge the courage
of one last beer.

JANIS IAN WAS RIGHT

A bulletin-board solar system taught
me the names of the planets, but Frankie
Avalon taught me the Goddess of Love.
Taught me love was for the blonde and
blue-eyed, not a Janis Ian girl like me
with cat's-eye glasses and no curves.

Frankie's girl had stars in her eyes
but I could never find them in mine,
just as I never found a man who would be true
though they swore it just like Frankie did.

But I do believe.

Not in romance from a record but in the deep,
dependable caring of the cosmos. When Venus
sits low to the horizon on a pale peach morning
or over the Pacific on one of those gold-streaked
autumn evenings, the tender washes over me.

WHAT I KNOW OF CORPSES

WHAT I KNOW OF CORPSES

I am eleven. Billy, my best friend's brother, just seven
when he darts out between parked cars on a rainy afternoon.
In the open casket, little man in suit and tie, rosy cheeks,
rosy lips, not the giggler in cowboy jammies with tuna
on his breath.

I am sixteen when Violet's flopping heart fails. My father
weeps buckets for his mom, but my eyes are dry, searching
her face for any sign of the line leader of grandma love.

At fifty-seven, I hold my father's blue-veined hand
as Morpheus blesses his exit. I watch his spirit slip
the hook and slide out into that dark pool beyond the stream.

This morning, I scoop Frannie up in the net of love
as the vet glides her over the last rapids. Honoring
our contract of catch-and-release, I lay her stillness
in the fleece-lined creel.

CAT GAMBLING

Cat love comes with
a stacked deck,
marked cards,
loaded dice.
The House of Styx
impossible to beat.

REQUIEM FOR REINIE

I roll my grief through airport security where
the shrapnel in my heart goes undetected.
I buckle my grief into the empty middle seat
where the woman at the window doesn't
notice, tossing her jean jacket over it.

I slip my best memory into the seat
pocket for safe keeping, the one
of the tiny ball of kitten loose in my lap
on the first drive home, not knowing he
would be my soul mate.

I feed my grief pretzels and Ritz crackers,
let it sip from my diet coke, choke back tears
when it pushes against my throat at 32,000 feet,
beats its paws against my chest.

I am flying my red eyes to Nashville,
anguish only abated by knowing I stayed
present the night before as he shifted
into the last sleep, eyes open to
whatever awaits us all.

WHAT EVIE LEFT ME

I see them scattered about, the shards of our years:
a fuzzy pink ball, a forgotten piece of kibble, a bit
of black fur, a jagged hole near her favorite sleep spot.

My heart broke early. Test results can do that. After
that, I had the courage but nothing I could change.
The virus had all the power.

Slowly the seeds of loss are taking root. The fissures
widen. My grief falls out through my fingers. Each
familiar thing I touch turns sharp as I pick up
the pieces of my heart.

I never get good at this.

THE DEAD EN ROUTE

I drive into the forest mid-morning,
following the ribbon from city to coast.
The sky July blue in April, the clouds
marshmallow white. Although the summer's
come early, the leaves still wear soft gowns.

I sail on smooth pavement through this sea
of trunks and limbs, happy, at peace, until
around the far curve comes the lumbering
hearse with its dozen dead.

I feel the hearts of the trees clench,
branches bow in sorrow for their friends,
their family. The truck rushes by carrying
toilet paper, envelopes, fence posts.

AFTER THE PARENTS GO HOME TO GRIEVE

The city sparkles in the wee-hour dark.
Jessica lies in my arms, here in this
chintz-padded rocker, the rise and fall
of her little lungs the only sign of life.

Six weeks since witnessing her first
moments and my friends' love, newly born.
Then a visitor, unannounced, brought
her tender brain to a standstill.

First babysitting. I was 11. Infant
cried for hours. I walked, sang, fed,
diapered. No avail. By the fourth
hour, I knew I wouldn't have my own.

I take my turn, as friends do.

A nurse takes Jessica from me,
blankets her body, swaddles the
soft, swollen skull. I stand, stretch,
move closer to the night.

My watch is in my pocket. I leave it there.

ON THE WAY FROM SAN JOSE

The airport's broken-down wing is tucked away
by short-term parking. A lone gate, a lone attendant.
I take a solo seat, a dun plastic chair long past
its prime. At my feet a black carry-on of loss.

A flock of flamingo girls swarms in, awash in
diesel fumes and hair gel. Pink satin shorts
and numbered team tanks. They twitter, joke,
jostle. Terminally restless.

I traveled solo with him once. Drove at night.
Jazz on the radio. Nothing to say. No flamingo
I. Instead a gawky chick, just hatched, with
an absentee father I barely knew.

The girls go in and out but I sit pinned to my
sorrow. Out the window, a sign says *No Stopping*.
Dad, dear now, is in a coma. Both of us
hurrying home.

THE LAST VIGIL

I left the hospital at midnight, crossed
the Interstate Bridge, then up silent Belmont.
I lay down with the cats, hoping three
grieving hours would bring me an open
heart to my father's last day.

Now in the dim melancholy of the ICU,
machines beep and whir, the modern grim reapers.
I sit on one side, my niece on the other. Hold
his hands, talk of love. Ours for him, his for us.

A few minutes past five, a hush descends. His
energy expands, fills the room, fills us,
solid and diffuse, sacred and ordinary.
Death's invitation, waiting on the dawn.

REPARATION

My mother's mind departed years
before my first sober breath. No
chance to join minds, amend hearts.

I tossed my needs, unsaid, into
a box, locked them in the attic
of feigned indifference.

The last morning, in her beige cage
of care, she refused touch, knew me not.
We both headed out empty, the train
of reconciliation long gone.

Days passed. Cold rain. Charcoal skies.

One noon I took my walk to the park. Just over
the second rise, time held its breath.
I looked up.

The ancient cedars knew me, knew my grief.
A feathered wind wafted me up, set me down,
seen, loved, repaired.

I NEVER TALKED TO MY MOTHER ABOUT HEAVEN

In my youth, she believed. Took us to church. Honored
the dead. Visited her infant's ashes. I believed too.
Then college. Then cynical. I lived for the moment.

In my 30s, she didn't go anymore. Never mentioned
Jesus. Never saw a Bible in her hands. By then, we both
worshipped the bottle. She never found a way out. I did.

What little we talked about didn't include divine solace,
though I hope she had some in those years of sundown
decline. That's what religion is for, isn't it?

Me, I'm not sure. I like that it's a mystery. And I know
I could watch forever the grace-filled limbs of the alders
in a windy sky.

WOMEN KNOW THESE THINGS

What Kitchen Ants Want

Things We Keep

Yoko in the Locker Room

To the Man Who Tried to Abduct Me

The Complication of Mothers

Craig's List: **Black kitten. Free**

You Once Asked Me to Plan Your Funeral

Famine of the Ancestors

Women's Weekend March 2011

When You Knew It Might Happen

Checking in to Anonymity

Never Too Old to Be a Mermaid

WHAT KITCHEN ANTS WANT

I want an easy entrance,
a clear crack between floor and door,
a loose line between pipe and board.

I want an easy assignment,
something tasty like a smear
of that apple cider from last Sunday.

I want quiet in the workplace,
no screams, no curses.
Look, lady, we all have a job to do.

I want clear messages from coworkers.
I don't want to show up when the picnic's over
and Lysol's all that's left.

Mostly, I want to step out of line,
wear a red beret,
blaze my own trail.
Following isn't all it's cracked up to be.

THINGS WE KEEP

The cups were bright blue, this side
of turquoise, smooth to the touch.
Their tulip curves pleased the hand,
their thin lips pleased the mouth.

The potter at the market was
even more magnificent:
honey skin, dark beard, dark eyes,
and *Oh!* his hands.

I circled back three times to that booth.
Half-brazen in those days, I took his
card and four cups, pretended not to see
the gold band on his slim finger.

That attic apartment with its nameless lovers,
the bright apple blossom mornings, coffee
in those blue cups. Only one is left, chipped,
cracked, its handle long gone.

YOKO IN THE LOCKER ROOM

You kept your coat on,
held your purse like an old auntie,
wore the perfume of inscrutability,
harbored otherness as if it were a pearl.

How did you not choke
on the boredom, on the resentment
of those boys who were still boys
even though they played in the majors.

Instead, you kept them from
flicking towels,
rehashing the game,
sneaking a peek
at each other's equipment.

You took up so little space
but you were still the Asian
elephant in the room.

TO THE MAN WHO TRIED TO ABDUCT ME

I smell you first. Your cigarette breath
on the back of my neck, your sour sweat.

Get in the car, bitch. Rush of fear.
I step out of myself. For I know. We all know.

We don't want to be Molly, raped by a highway
patrolman on a rural road. Or Sarah, raped by
the bagboy from Piggly Wiggly.

I also know to do this: Throw the keys under the car.

You bitch! You push me to the parking strip, onto the grass.
Cuff my head. It's just what I need to come back into me.
A harpy. A screech owl. You're gone.

Two girls help me up the stairs, give me water, call 911.
Patrolman comes with his notepad. *I never saw his face.*
Shakes his head, closes his notebook.

A month goes by. I'm walking home from Hiron's Drugstore
with tampons and three Snickers. I pass you.

Don't recognize the jeans, the sleeveless tee, the unwashed
hair. Only the miasma of violence, of misogyny.

I don't call the police. I know the memory of a smell won't be
enough, no matter how much it stays with us.

THE COMPLICATION OF MOTHERS

A thin blonde with a bad haircut and the reedy
bones of nicotine and diet soda has the middle
seat. I smile and take the aisle. She nods at
the withered woman at the window. *My mom,
moving up from Phoenix.* Her mouth purses
with a bitterness as old as the Bible.

The mom helps herself to Cheetos from the
daughter's tray, shows us scraps
of balled-up tissues with mumbled meanings.
The daughter shakes her head, looks at her watch.

I try to picture you at the window, me in the middle.
My heart still yearning, your mind
vacant as the sky.

CRAIG'S LIST: *BLACK KITTEN. FREE.*

The Giver

The woman is prompt, I'll say that for her, and she finds us, which isn't always easy. I make Jack turn the wrestling down, make the kids shut up with their carrying on. Tanya clings to the kitten. Billy blubbers that it belongs to him. *We can't keep it.* How many times do I have to tell them?

She looks nice enough, older than I expected, retired probably—wonder what that's like. But her car isn't fancy, no newer than ours, just washed. She wants to know its name. I'm too embarrassed to say that it's Shazam. She wants to know its age. Does she want it or not?

I'm not happy to let that little bit of softness go, but I can tell she'll give it food and a home, more than we can do.

The Receiver

A part of Portland I don't know: gravel alleys, pot-hole puddles. The address invisible, then a garage with magic marker numbers. A woman answers my knock. Scraggly hair, junk-food pallor. She carries him out, pushes him towards me: long-haired, half-grown, gold eyes of Egypt.

I ask simple questions. She's curt, sharp with me. But I know it isn't anger. I can see despair, tears right behind.

I smile. *I'll take him.*

Something loosens her jaw a little. She looks at a point across the street. *We're being evicted.*

I give that half-smile of sorrow, the one that's barely better than nothing. At the car, the kitten slips into the carrier without complaint as if he too knows.

I look over at the woman watching. She dips her chin. Goes into the garage, leaves the door open. An old sofa, stuffing coming out. Overstuffed trash bags, clothes spilling onto the concrete floor.

YOU ONCE ASKED ME TO PLAN YOUR FUNERAL

over green tea and pad thai. We were tight-knit then.
Thick as thieves. The acolytes, the adoration still to come.

Our unraveling was slow. You became the One in our gathering
of seekers. Your word the Word. Disciple didn't fit me.

Now one wall: a larger-than-life you in your Buddhist robe.
The community center packed with flowers and saintly praises.
Weeping followers. Solemn testimonials. No words about

the naughty girl who helped me write curse-word limericks
over curry at Thanh Thao, who took me to that sex shop
on Sandy where we bought trinkets for each other.

She's the one I miss.

FAMINE OF THE ANCESTORS

Up the desolate Doo Lough Valley, we stop at an enormous Celtic cross, memorial to the Great Famine. 1847. A village's worth of Irish peasants dragged their starvation twelve miles down this road to the manor house. The English lord refused to see them. His luncheon could not be disturbed.

May wind is bitter, clouds scudding across the sky.
Most died on the way home.

Two days earlier. The Dingle Peninsula. Blue sky, meringue clouds. We drove by a stone hut up a hillside. *Famine Cottage. Visit 5 Euros.* We stopped. My friend got out. I couldn't. A paralysis of ancestry pinned me to the seat. I could feel the suffering from where I sat.

Tonight we will shop for food in a market of possibilities my famine-scarred forebears could not have dreamed of. I think of my own struggles with food, wonder if that desperation is in my DNA.

WOMEN'S WEEKEND MARCH 2011

Sirens wail just before six. Nervous inlanders, we hustle up
the hill to the Church of St Peter with its fish nets and folding
chairs. No mermaid voices call us, just a taped message
on a megaphone urging us to higher ground.

The sea on our side is steel grey and winter high, the rain
bone cold. People stand around in the soaking mist, watching
the waves, speculating. We know next to nothing on this
Friday. We've left belongings and cars at the weekend rental.

On our side, zero hour comes and goes with waves that look
familiar to Oregon storm watchers. Only the tide, sucked
out for long eerie moments, hints at what has happened.
We go back down, relieved that our weekend has not
washed away.

TV tells us Fukushima is reeling from a heave in the plates,
rushing the sea in and the bodies out, beginning the atoms'
decay. Safe, warm, we watch the wall of water surge, writhe.
Grieve for all that will never be the same. Exhausted, we fall
into dry beds on dry land, gratitude our blanket, sorrow
our pillow.

WHEN YOU KNEW IT MIGHT HAPPEN

No trail, no map, the way ahead into the woods
unknown. We go on walking, the talk too
precious to lose, like your breast.

Later, leaning against the headboard, you read
from the *Tibetan Book of the Dead,* tell me
to hold your death lightly should it come now.

Thirty years more we've had. You on your
coast, I on mine. That moment of love
crisp and clear in my heart.

CHECKING IN TO ANONYMITY

Sometimes you drive by a nice hotel, the kind with a
uniformed parking valet, and you want to pull over, check
in, take the elevator to the third floor. A hushed hallway
leads to 306, its solid door opens to a spacious room, a view
of lives you've not taken.

Zen-clean surfaces. High thread-count linens. In the closet
two soft cotton shirts, fitted black pants, that perfect red
jacket you've never found. In the bathroom, a silk kimono,
enough shampoo and cucumber lotion for a week.

On the nightstand a new novel, a book of poems you
haven't read in years. On the desk six sharp pencils, a little
sketchbook, a pocket journal.

Two, three, four days ahead
     as empty as the drawers
of the polished dresser.

NEVER TOO OLD TO BE A MERMAID

I stand in the deeper end. Push off,
hoping legs, arms, breath find each other.
The rhythm is jerky as a marionette. I
can't hold stroke, breath, kick in my mind.
No muscle memory yet.

I'm eight. A motel pool. I belly flop
after reluctant dives. Dad pulls me out
to sit on the side. I don't dive again.

I'm twelve. Camp on a river. Step into a deep
hole. Panic. The lifeguard pulls me out to sit
on the side. I can't put my head under again.

I'm seventy-three. Ready to learn. I hang
on to the side, face in, blowing bubbles.

I'm seventy-six. Stand in the deeper end.
Push off, body all in, goggled eyes open.
Jerky. Uncoordinated. Fearless.

MARRIED TO THE MUSE

Married to the Muse

Ode to My First Magician

Chère Simone

William Carlos Williams in My Attic

The Old Lady and the Teacup

Bridal Path

MARRIED TO THE MUSE

In my youth, my body found love. My heart
did not. I chose the man with the wandering eye

over and over. With the last heartbreak
I came to my senses: sight, touch, color.

The muse reached for me then. Offered
steady satisfaction, a troth to deep

connection, joy, delight in the
written page, the painted board.

How could I say no.

ODE TO MY FIRST MAGICIAN

Doris is home, back from wherever she goes.
    Soft black pants, Chinese satin slippers,
        a loose blouse of white silk.

She smiles, crystal glass of bourbon
    in hand, tender look just for me,
        just twelve, blossoming here.

Are you writing? I nod, a fresh poem in my pocket.
    May I see? I fidget, leave it there.
        I'll send it to you.

Last time I was here, I wandered
    the modern house, cantilevered over
        Portland. Admired netsuke artfully placed,

blue vase of white peonies, white rugs, white walls.
    No chintz like at home, no floral papers,
        no early American secrets.

I don't know this is the last time. Don't know that
    the loose blouse covers a swollen liver,
        the long times away are for drying out.

Don't know I too will be lured by bourbon,
    become addicted to bad boys,
        dance with the reaper.

Don't know I will get a second life,
    make a Zen-spacious home,
        explore the worlds housed in words.

CHÈRE SIMONE

Mind if I call you that? I feel I know you.
Read you in 1970 in that lonely Texas
office where I temped for six tedious months.

Read *Le Deuxième Sexe.* Both volumes! *En français!*
Kept them hidden in the desk drawer. Read when
no one was watching. You rocked my world!

My mother shared your birth date.
Quelle coincidence! Her hemmed-in life
so unlike yours. No *égalité*. No *liberté*.

I too was a dutiful daughter but you
taught me to say no. No to housewife
confinement, to a child-burdened life.

I never found a Sartre, wrong time, wrong
place. But the pill brought *liberté, égalité,*
if not true love, and I struck out on my own

like you. When I took to writing myself
as the hero of my life, your books, your photo
sat on the desk before me.

WILLIAM CARLOS WILLIAMS IN MY ATTIC

The flashlight beams up inches of dust,
the house fifty years if it's a day. I hunch
into the low space, brush away fat strings
of cobweb, come upon treasures.

Maple bed frame for the mattress now on the
bedroom floor. Tall flask of clear turquoise,
a window jewel for the breakfast sun. Poster
tube nearly missed in the thick dust.

I tease out a short roll of fine vellum
tied with purple satin, a poem neatly penned
in a flowing script. I hang the spell of its magic
on the raspberry wall of my kitchen.

Plums over the icebox. So sweet!

THE OLD LADY AND THE TEA CUP

Crisp dawn of winter.
No sailors here to take warning,
just an old woman with black tea
in a blue and white cup, its rounded
body warm in her hands.

The evergreens toward the park
etch their tips against the red rise.
Then in a blink or five, the crimson has pinked,
Homer's verse of rosy-fingered dawn welling
up from some long-ago learning.

The light begins to blue the sky. The tea
cools for drinking. She leaves the window
with its view to the coming day, sits at the table
with its bee-gold cloth, and writes.

BRIDAL PATH

On her way home from work, she comes
upon a half-spelled word, a rainbow,
a unicorn smudged by a sprinkler. In the
corner of the stairs, fat pastel cylinders
the color of wedding mints in tiny paper cups.

She never had a wedding with those little mints,
only the dress, Brazilian lace and river cloth. Bought
when the love was already fading. No Miss Haversham,
she chose to walk away when fidelity wasn't on the table.

Now she heads home, picks up her own
soft chalks: cerulean scarlet magenta gold.
Smooth as a bride waltzing with her father,
she marries the pressed powder to the page.

NEIGHBORHOOD WATCH

97 Chevy Malibu

Mid-August at the Mall

*The Goddess at the Entrance
to the Ross Island Bridge*

Ode to Betty from the Gym

Neighborhood Cronies

Sunday Early: The Hour of the Crow

97 CHEVY MALIBU

Sleeping bag sags out the passenger window.
Zipper's split off from the cowboy lining.
August heat wave. Day 3.

Jeans, high tops, dinosaur underpants heaped
in the backseat, Batman action figure on top.
A grimy stuffed Dalmatian rides the back window ledge.

Stale smoke and wet flannel walk me down
to the corner, hoping love is travelling with them
and not just the dilemma of milk, cigarettes, or laundromat.

MID-AUGUST AT THE MALL

She's one row over and two tables down near Orange Julius.
Two baggy sweaters, polyester slacks cinched with twine.
Her companions: two bulging black garbage bags.
On the table: greasy paper bag, plastic cup from Taco Time.

I'm wearing capris, t-shirt, sandals.
My companion: leather briefcase.
On the table: chicken teriyaki, ice water, laptop.

For the next three hours I edit important passages
in important documents. Eat more than I need.
She sits in the orange plastic chair, wipes her nose
on a blue bandana, sips from the Taco Time cup,
mumbles to herself.

I agonize.
Offer her the rest of my lunch.
Take her home.
Give her a bed for the night.
I don't.

The next day I give a $10 bill to a one-legged man
at a freeway exit.

THE GODDESS AT THE ENTRANCE
TO THE ROSS ISLAND BRIDGE

When she stands up to take the twenty,
her height, her heft are from Diego Rivera.
Skin the warm sand we whites kill ourselves to get.

No Amazon bow at the breast but a toddler. Her
battle as fierce as any myth.

ODE TO BETTY FROM THE GYM

Six feet and statuesque in lumberjack flannel, low-rider
jeans. Caramel skin, tight gray curls. A snake of a scar on
her wrist. She always staked out the hip extender machine,
read grocery circulars and *The Inquirer* between sets.

She'd call me over from my struggles at the sit-up bench,
show me celebrity shenanigans, ridiculous recipes,
impossible prices for chicken thighs or pork loin.

The owner said she'd been a cop. I could see it. She had
a way, a no bullshit scowl she turned on the wannabe
Mr. Americas who dropped too-heavy weights with a bang.

She seemed immortal. Then a stroke. Then one of those
places no one wants to go. Then gone.

If there's a gym in heaven, Betty's there four mornings a
week, our gym bag and circulars in hand. At ours, the hip
extender now has a bronze plaque: **The Betty.**

NEIGHBORHOOD CRONIES

A gaunt *nonna* from *The Godfather* crosses Sandy
Boulevard as I wait for the green. Widow black. Brown
50s pocketbook over one arm. Only bright spot a cotton
kerchief with red roses.

Other crones are familiar. A round Russian in striped skirt
and plaid sweater pulling a little cart past my house. A
Korean woman with crimson hair, crimson lipstick on her
way to the 7-11 each noon. But I don't recognize this crow
of a woman collaged onto Sandy with its cannabis billboards
and Subaru traffic.

It's a long light. I look down at my lavender t-shirt, my
trendy crop pants, my khaki Skechers. I smile at her. Old
ladies both.

SUNDAY EARLY: THE HOUR OF THE CROW

6:08 I slow for two breakfasting on
a splay of crackers, on a squirrel who
didn't make it across.

6:12 I notice one on a wire,
watching a woman in a frayed
track suit pushing a walker,
dragging a leg, her body an isosceles.

6:15 A scattered murder up ahead eyes
young vagabonds. Backpacks for cushions.
Fast food wrappers.

6:24. Home again. Reggie and Talullah,
corvids in residence, saunter down my driveway.

I WROTE A POEM OF LONELINESS

Winter Sunday in France

Witness Protection

Usually When It Comes

A Bold Move

Bashō Said It Well

I Wrote a Poem of Loneliness

WINTER SUNDAY IN FRANCE

A pathetic zoo. A cramped cage off the beaten path.
I speak to him in English, my comfort, maybe his.

Weekdays have cafés, libraries, the *supermarché*.
Sundays nothing, no one.

He listens patiently to the shame of my desolate days
drenched in wine, the staggering lonesome I'm trapped in.

How I got here is a tedious story.
Why I have stayed so long a character flaw.

The park is deserted. It's always deserted.
Just me and the raccoon, a *raton laveur américain*.

I stay till I'm chilled to the bone.

WITNESS PROTECTION

I've never been a fan of Tom Hanks—
superficial, facile, that damn box of chocolates.
But lately I've been thinking about my mother.
How she couldn't witness her own life, let alone mine.
How we perish slowly if our spikes and saves
go unnoticed by our teammates.
How we need someone to hold up the net.
How even a volley ball can keep us
from dying of loneliness.

USUALLY WHEN IT COMES

my fear rumbles like a slow freight,
takes its time through the intersection
of illogic and nerves.

Twice though, it's sped up, careening
down the tracks toward my body tied
to the rails and no hero in sight.

I slipped the cords of memory then,
ghosted the self who couldn't come
to her senses, rested between cars
on the train of my life.

I don't know what called me back,
some silent whistle of safety perhaps,
but it did.

A BOLD MOVE

Learning to love without fear
takes a screwdriver, metal shears,
someone to loosen the armor,
not keep it shiny and well oiled.

Learning to love without fear
takes a Swiss Army blade to cut
the ties, slit the tape. Gentle hands
to fold the paper back, pry the lid
off the gift.

BASHŌ SAID IT WELL

It's harder to be old in spring.
My spirit is building a new nest
but my body limps and frets.

The old lilac has sparse limbs
but the deep purple blooms
are as fragrant as ever.

Weathered bones on my mind.
Worn bones in my body.
Age is speaking my name.

I WROTE A POEM OF LONELINESS

Not much of a poem. A clenched
heart unsure of opening. No
sobbing, weeping. Not my way.
Just pushed-down sorrow.

But oh, the morning! A few wisps
of white in the blue, the birds riotous,
the lavender wafting loveliness as the
bumble bees swing on the blooms,
the sprinkler teasing the leaves
of the mock orange, Sammy
curled at my feet.

HOW MAGIC COMES

God Lives for Me in Trees

Dream Boats

Sister Doe

Shinrin-Yoku

Flying North from Sacramento

Shooting Star

The Trappist Abbey

Sacred Sightings

The Gypsy

GOD LIVES FOR ME IN TREES

The early morning loved me best, the bell
summoning us to silence. We gathered
our energy, stilled our young voices.
There was prayer but I didn't listen,
already not my way. The young pastor
blessed us, scattered us onto
the wide green grounds.

I was anxious, afraid another would
take my spot, but each day the tree was
waiting for me. I read the verse out of good
girl, closed my eyes, leaned against
the strong life behind me.

Quiet around me.
Quiet inside me.
The real church of church camp.

DREAM BOATS

We spend the afternoon gathering moss, leaves, blossoms.
Glue them to a plank of bark. Chatter like young squirrels.
We stay up into summer dark, campfire-singing *Kumbaya*,
My Paddle's Keen and Bright. Pass around s'mores.

We quiet. Start down the path, counselors softly
singing *WoHeLo*. Hear a snapped twig. Stop at
the call of a great horned owl. The bank of the
broad creek, unfamiliar in the dark.

A hush falls, deeper than church. Matches flare.
Candles, wax-welded to the small slabs, begin
to glow.

I hold my breath, feel the holiness of the bark boats
as they take float, some hesitating, some eager to go.
Watch my dreams move on, downstream.

SISTER DOE

She steps out from the trees onto the broad lawn.
Ear twitches, hoof scratches cheek.
She looks over at me, eyes soft, open.
Holds my gaze. I smile. Her heads bows
to a green breakfast.

I sigh my stillness, feel my ribs open and
close as hers push out the thick scar
across her side. I breathe love in
her direction, bow to our beating hearts.

She doesn't bolt when I leave my cushion
for warm tea and this poem. I let that
trust carry me through the day, both of us
held in the peace of this place.

SHINRIN-YOKU

I stand in the forest at dawn,
breathing, bathing, the air
heavy laden with Spirit. Dew
descends from branch and leaf,
a baptism.

I lean into the spine of an old alder,
its bark scratching my back,
Grandma's fingers through my t-shirt,
my head in her lap. Resting in touch.

FLYING NORTH FROM SACRAMENTO

We may have been the only ones
to see the light, the cowboy
in the next seat and I. Gold orange
to the west like fresh squeezed juice
over a wide swath of the horizon.

It's got to be the ocean, he said,
that shine down there on the water,
but we were flying right up the Valley,
Cascade peaks to our right, Eugene,
then Salem massed beneath us.

Fog, we decided, lying over the Coast Range,
its crystal drops reflecting the last of the day,
guiding us home.

SHOOTING STAR

You might have missed it.

You might have hurried to the shower
house near Diamond Hall, eyes downcast
to gift others their solitude. Or you might
have scurried out the door to your room,
eager to be free of the rabbit holes your brain
lured you down during the hours of *sesshin*.

Instead, you lingered, practiced mindful movement—
folded the green chenille blanket,
straightened your cushions,
bowed to Buddha and Kwan Yin.
Made your measured way out of the hall,
took care in buttoning the black fleece jacket,
struggling your shoes over the green-striped socks.

You joined me then, stepped off the covered porch,
breathed deep of pine, of night chill. Looked up.

THE TRAPPIST ABBEY

Three days of cool October sun.
Three nights of a narrow penitent's bed.
Three nights of the full moon silvering.
the pond, silvering my naked body when
I throw off the sheets.

Five services of song and supplication.
No meals worth lingering over.
Silence hard to hold on to,
the inner voices loud even when
I throw back the sheets.

Yet something is soothed under that cool sun.
No need to pry the fingers of anxiety off my soul.
Instead, an open-handed surrender.

SACRED SIGHTINGS

Saw Joseph, Mary, and Jesus in the parking lot at Trader Joe's.
The Madonna held a shawl over her head and the child's,
the Father held a cardboard sign but I'd left home without
my wallet so I blessed them and hurried on.

Saw God pushing a shopping cart of cans past my driveway.
He hadn't bathed in forever. A cigarette drooped from his lip
and he gave me a look of hurt and hate so hard I went back
to my car for an offering of socks but he'd moved on.

Saw the Devil on every Sunday channel, pitching for
pity, schilling for old folks' savings, smarm and greed
and lust incarnate. I turned away with contempt and
changed the channel.

Heard the Holy Spirit singing its heart out from a tree
in first leaf, no bigger than a minute, so full of hope
and joy at being alive that I took heart, load lightened,
dreams shimmering in that first light.

THE GYPSY

A long way from town, she says as she comes
in from the rain. I offer a towel but her clothes,
her hair are desert-dry. I open my mind to ask
but she sits down, lays her cards on the table.
Pick three, she says.

The first is white and blank. She points to
a dot so small I would never have seen it.
Your problems, she says.

The second is the green of woods, ferns, moss.
Step in, she says. I hear the day owl hoot and a stream
sing its tune. The cool of the trees lies easy on my shoulders.
Your heart's home, she says.

The third is the bruised blue of sky birthing a storm.
Shelter here, she says. *It's where the power lies.*

I ALSO LOVE THE LITTLE THINGS

Love Letter on My Walk

Light on the Diagonal

Quiet of the Peony

Ode to the Outdoor Shower

October Saturday on Mt Hood

One More Dance

In the Early, I Call to My Dreams

I Also Love the Little Things

LOVE LETTER ON MY WALK

Shadows branch-cast,
pavement the paper.
Sun holds the pen,
writes to me.

I can't read the script
yet I know what it is
to be loved by the world
when spring comes.

LIGHT ON THE DIAGONAL

Early sun after days of Biblical rain.
Mid-May and near freezing at night.
Heat's on.

Frannie sprawls across my journal, can't
get close enough this morning. Everything
feels tender. Her need. My love.

The celery green leaves rustle on the paper bark
maple. An avian Pavarotti practices the scales.

Josie curls up in a patch of sun. The window
casing slides its shadow across the magenta rug.

QUIET OF THE PEONY

I bought some on Sunday,
magenta peeking from the tight buds.
Full blooms tempted me,
but I wanted the whole show,
the slow unfolding.

Peonies look demure in the bud,
shy, closed in upon themselves
like the lonely girl serving punch at the prom,
but get that peony out on the dance floor
and she goes all twirly skirts.

ODE TO THE OUTDOOR SHOWER

I watch the light dance in the leaves
from my wooden perch. Hot water flows
down my back, cool breeze flutters my skin.

Naked to the marsh, I am seen
only by a robin flitting into the trees,
a mosquito singing with blood lust.

OCTOBER SATURDAY ON MT HOOD

Dawn stitches the mountain into its pale self.
No hints of rosy fingers, no tinge of pink or peach.
The old firs quilt their triangle tops onto the black
blanket below while the alders along the river
powder their dusky green noses. The hovering
fog moves downstream.

I follow a sun-ray road across the meadow.
The trip is brief, the way narrow. Chased by
oak shadows, I'm picking up seed hitchers
with every step, my socks a cargo van.

ONE MORE DANCE

Some bumbles still come
to the lavender
hoping to hook up
like the drunk and lonely at last call.

The host of stalks with their pale
purple dresses have dried out, gone
on Nature's wagon, though a few
fresh beauties still dance and flirt.

But the big summer party is over,
the apian gents heading home to the hive.

IN THE EARLY, I CALL TO MY DREAMS

I go to bed early these days
tired of the light, of myself by nine,
preferring the cool arrival of day,
the small blessings of bird talk.

In the early, I move slow, sit
long minutes after meditation,
think of nothing,
wait patiently for the tea to cool,
watch steam waft across the cup,
blue-glazed.

In the early, I soak up beauty,
watch the bushtits go out to breakfast,
watch the cloud wisps dawdle, in no
hurry to cross the sky.

I ALSO LOVE THE LITTLE THINGS

The tiny pink stars of phlox massing against brick.
The single cat whisker left on the sofa.
The vibration of the hummer when he visits the geranium.
The one sly streak of hot pink under the gray cloud.
The last sip of tea from the cup Judith gave me.
The one tulip that never opened.
The sliver of soap with the scent of ripe mango.
The pennies in the gym parking lot.

A NOTE FROM THE AUTHOR

I dabbled in poetry for a few years but when the pandemic lockdown came, I started writing a poem every day to express my fears and my loneliness. At about the same time, I began taking photos of my neighborhood on my daily walks and posting them online. Both practices have been so wonderful that I've kept them up.

Creative practices have endless variety, endless things to learn and try, so much satisfaction to be had in the doing. Marrying the muse was one of the best choices I ever made.

ACKNOWLEDGEMENTS

My thanks to my poetry buddies: Ginny Folger, Irene Brennan, Jeanne Hillson, Pat Topitizer, Tina Johnson, and especially to Susan Zimmerman for our many conversations. Thanks also to my teachers, Marj Hahne and Ellen Bass, for so much craft wisdom. And most especially, thank you to Sage Cohen, poetry partner extraordinaire, for her suggestions and support on this journey.

Jill Kelly is a poet, novelist, photographer, and painter. A former college professor and freelance editor, she came to her creative practices later in life. She lives in Portland, Oregon, with three feline assistants of the Muse. You can find more of her work at **jillkellycreative.com**.

Made in the USA
Monee, IL
20 May 2023

34119204R00070